WELCOME TO THE U.S.A.

IDAHO

Written by Ann Heinrichs   Illustrated by Matt Kania
Content Adviser: Jane Houston, Research Librarian,
Idaho State University, Boise, Idaho

The Child's World

Published in the United States of America by The Child's World®
PO Box 326 • Chanhassen, MN 55317-0326
800-599-READ • www.childsworld.com

Photo Credits
Cover: Idaho Tourism/Idaho Travel Council; frontispiece: Getty Images/The Image Bank/Chris Noble.

Interior: AP/Wide World Photos/Idaho State Journal/Bill Schaefer: 25; Corbis: 10 (Tim Thompson), 13 (James L. Amos), 26 (Mark E. Gibson), 29 (Roger Ressmeyer); Bryan Day/Basque Center: 21; Fort Hall Replica Commission: 17; Friends of the Idaho Historical Museum: 18; Idaho Tourism: 6 (Peg Owens), 14 (Sacajawea Center); Idaho Tourism/Idaho Travel Council: 9 (Jack Williams), 30 (Jas Krdzalic), 34 (Shelly DeMoss); Potlatch Corporation: 33; Sierra Silver Mine Tour: 22.

Acknowledgments
The Child's World®: Mary Berendes, Publishing Director

Editorial Directions, Inc.: E. Russell Primm, Editorial Director; Katie Marsico, Associate Editor; Judith Shiffer, Assistant Editor; Matt Messbarger, Editorial Assistant; Susan Hindman, Copy Editor; Melissa McDaniel, Proofreader; Kevin Cunningham, Peter Garnham, Matt Messbarger, Olivia Nellums, Chris Simms, Molly Symmonds, Katherine Trickle, Carl Stephen Wender, Fact Checkers; Tim Griffin/IndexServ, Indexer; Cian Loughlin O'Day, Photo Researcher and Editor
The Design Lab: Kathleen Petelinsek, Design; Julia Goozen, Art Production

Library of Congress Cataloging-in-Publication Data
Heinrichs, Ann.
   Idaho / by Ann Heinrichs ; cartography and illustrations by Matt Kania.
      p. cm. — (Welcome to the U.S.A.)
   Includes index.
   ISBN 1-59296-471-0 (library bound : alk. paper) 1. Idaho—Juvenile literature.
I. Kania, Matt, ill. II. Title.
   F746.3.H453 2006
   979.6–dc22   2005004812

Ann Heinrichs is the author of more than 100 books for children and young adults. She has also enjoyed successful careers as a children's book editor and an advertising copywriter. Ann grew up in Fort Smith, Arkansas, and lives in Chicago, Illinois.

**About the Author
Ann Heinrichs**

Matt Kania loves maps and, as a kid, dreamed of making them. In school he studied geography and cartography, and today he makes maps for a living. Matt's favorite thing about drawing maps is learning about the places they represent. Many of the maps he has created can be found in books, magazines, videos, Web sites, and public places.

**About the Map Illustrator
Matt Kania**

On the cover: **Run wild along the Snake River!**
On page one: **A snowboarder flies high at Sun Valley!**

OUR IDAHO TRIP

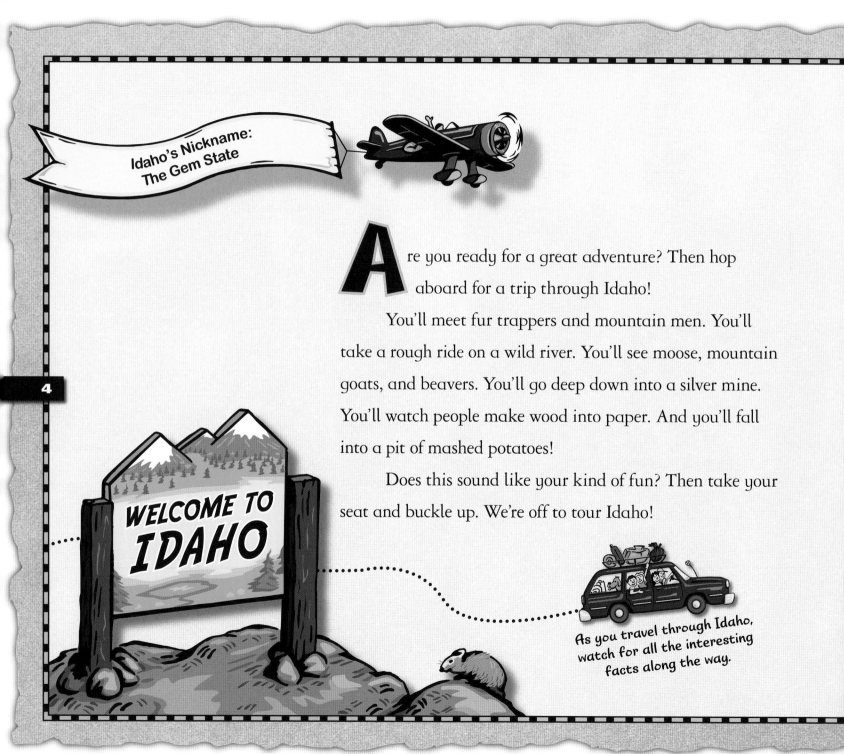

Idaho's Nickname:
The Gem State

Are you ready for a great adventure? Then hop aboard for a trip through Idaho!

You'll meet fur trappers and mountain men. You'll take a rough ride on a wild river. You'll see moose, mountain goats, and beavers. You'll go deep down into a silver mine. You'll watch people make wood into paper. And you'll fall into a pit of mashed potatoes!

Does this sound like your kind of fun? Then take your seat and buckle up. We're off to tour Idaho!

WELCOME TO IDAHO

As you travel through Idaho, watch for all the interesting facts along the way.

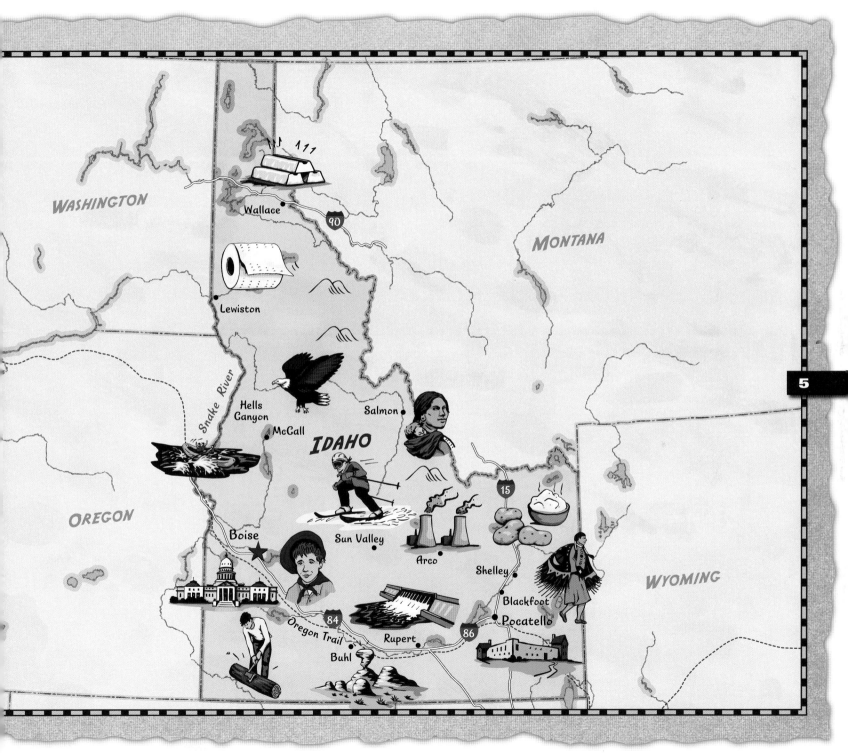

WASHINGTON

MONTANA

111

Wallace

90

Lewiston

Hells
Canyon

McCall

Salmon

IDAHO

15

OREGON

Boise

Sun Valley

Arco

Shelley

WYOMING

Blackfoot

Pocatello

84

Oregon Trail

Rupert

86

Buhl

Snake River

Grab your life jacket! It's time to raft through Hells Canyon.

Idaho's northernmost area is a narrow piece of land. It's called the Panhandle.

Boating through Hells Canyon

Whee! The waters rush and swirl around you. Curious animals watch from the riverbanks. Towering peaks rise overhead. You're racing through Hells Canyon! It's a deep **gorge** on the Snake River.

The Snake River is Idaho's major river. It crosses the southern part of the state. Then it forms part of the western border. That's where Hells Canyon is. The fields in the river plain are very fertile. They receive irrigation water from the river.

The Rocky Mountains cover northern and central Idaho. These rugged mountains are wild and beautiful. Many of them have snowcapped peaks all year long. Some of Idaho's wilderness areas have no roads.

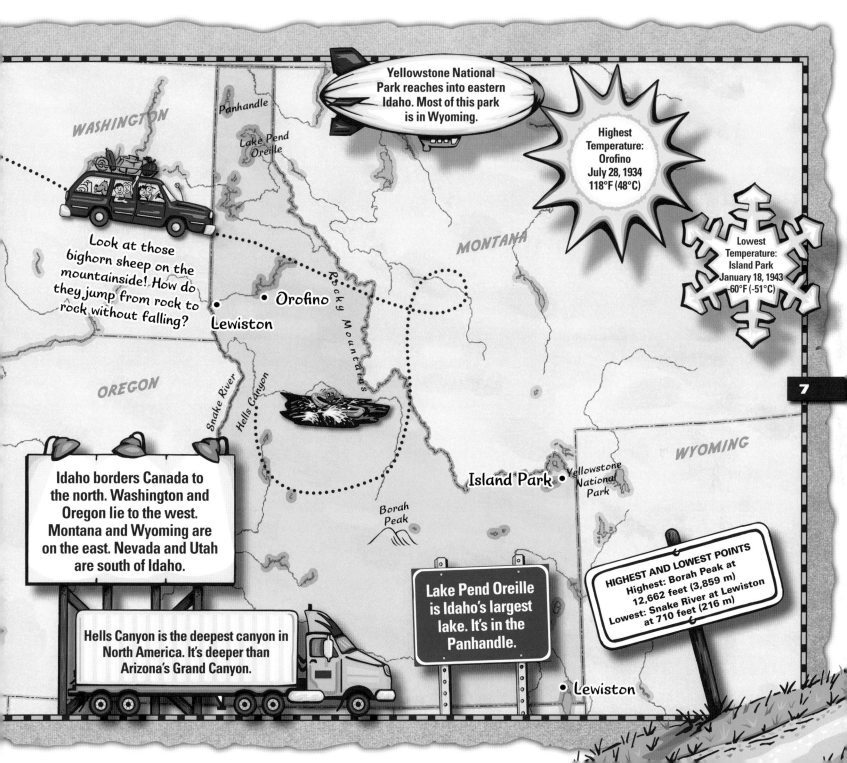

Yellowstone National Park reaches into eastern Idaho. Most of this park is in Wyoming.

Highest Temperature: Orofino July 28, 1934 118°F (48°C)

Lowest Temperature: Island Park January 18, 1943 -60°F (-51°C)

Look at those bighorn sheep on the mountainside! How do they jump from rock to rock without falling?

Idaho borders Canada to the north. Washington and Oregon lie to the west. Montana and Wyoming are on the east. Nevada and Utah are south of Idaho.

Hells Canyon is the deepest canyon in North America. It's deeper than Arizona's Grand Canyon.

Lake Pend Oreille is Idaho's largest lake. It's in the Panhandle.

HIGHEST AND LOWEST POINTS
Highest: Borah Peak at 12,662 feet (3,859 m)
Lowest: Snake River at Lewiston at 710 feet (216 m)

WASHINGTON
Panhandle
Lake Pend Oreille
MONTANA
Orofino
Lewiston
Rocky Mountains
OREGON
Snake River
Hells Canyon
Borah Peak
Island Park
Yellowstone National Park
WYOMING
Lewiston

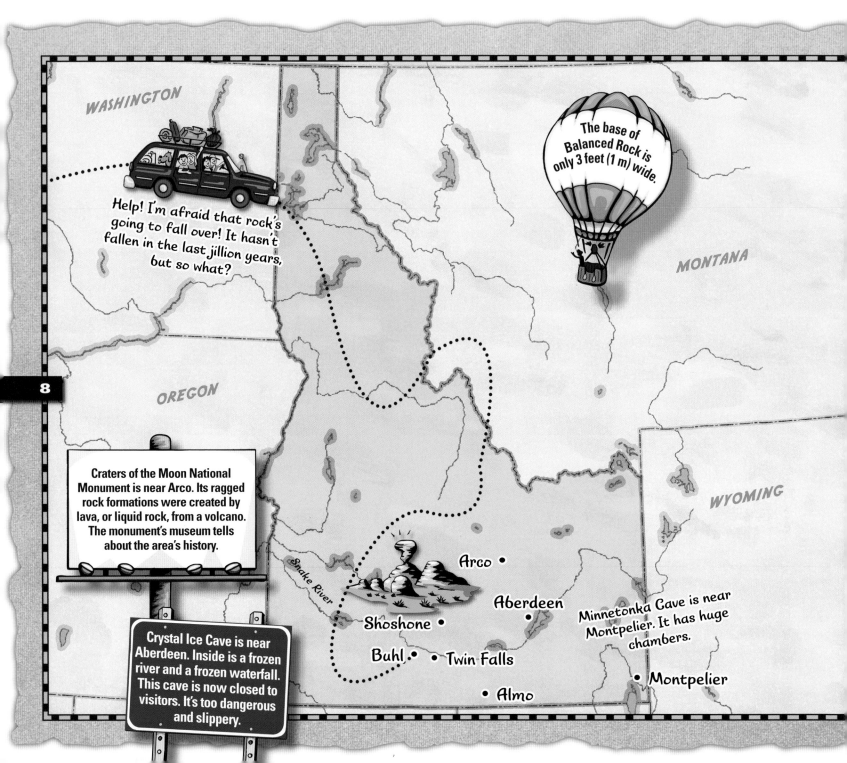

WASHINGTON

MONTANA

OREGON

WYOMING

The base of Balanced Rock is only 3 feet (1 m) wide.

Help! I'm afraid that rock's going to fall over! It hasn't fallen in the last jillion years, but so what?

Craters of the Moon National Monument is near Arco. Its ragged rock formations were created by lava, or liquid rock, from a volcano. The monument's museum tells about the area's history.

Crystal Ice Cave is near Aberdeen. Inside is a frozen river and a frozen waterfall. This cave is now closed to visitors. It's too dangerous and slippery.

Snake River

Arco •

• Aberdeen

Shoshone •

Minnetonka Cave is near Montpelier. It has huge chambers.

Buhl • • Twin Falls

• Montpelier

• Almo

Rocks, Caves, and Waterfalls

The giant rock looms high overhead. It weighs as much as ten elephants! But it balances on just a tiny base. It's the world-famous Balanced Rock near Buhl. The City of Rocks is another rocky wonder. This jumble of granite is near Almo. Its rocks are worn into many strange shapes.

Idaho has hundreds of underground caves. Shoshone Ice Caves are north of Shoshone. Their icy walls sparkle.

Lots of waterfalls tumble down Idaho's rocky cliffs. Shoshone Falls is on the Snake River near Twin Falls. Shoshone Indians called it "hurling waters leaping."

Want to see a natural wonder? Just visit the Balanced Rock near Buhl.

Shoshone Falls is higher than New York's Niagara Falls.

This hawk calls the skies above Idaho home.

10

The Birds of Prey Natural Conservation Area is south of Boise along the Snake River.

Listen for a high-pitched "eep!" sound. It's made by a rabbitlike animal called a pika. Look high on the rocky cliffs. You'll see mountain goats with nimble feet. Pass by a lake. Moose are standing knee-deep in the water. Beavers and otters are swimming nearby.

You're wandering through Payette National Forest. It's in central Idaho near McCall. This region has few people. That makes it a great home for wildlife.

Bird-watchers find a lot to watch in Idaho. Eagles, hawks, and falcons soar high overhead. Woodpeckers with bright red heads peck on forest trees. Down below, wild turkeys waddle along the ground.

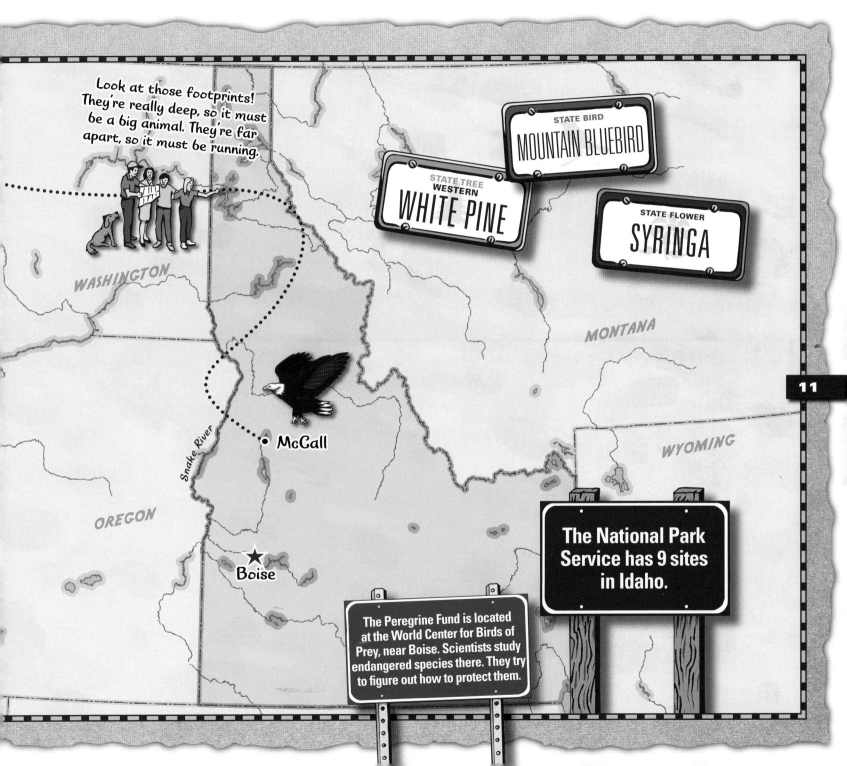

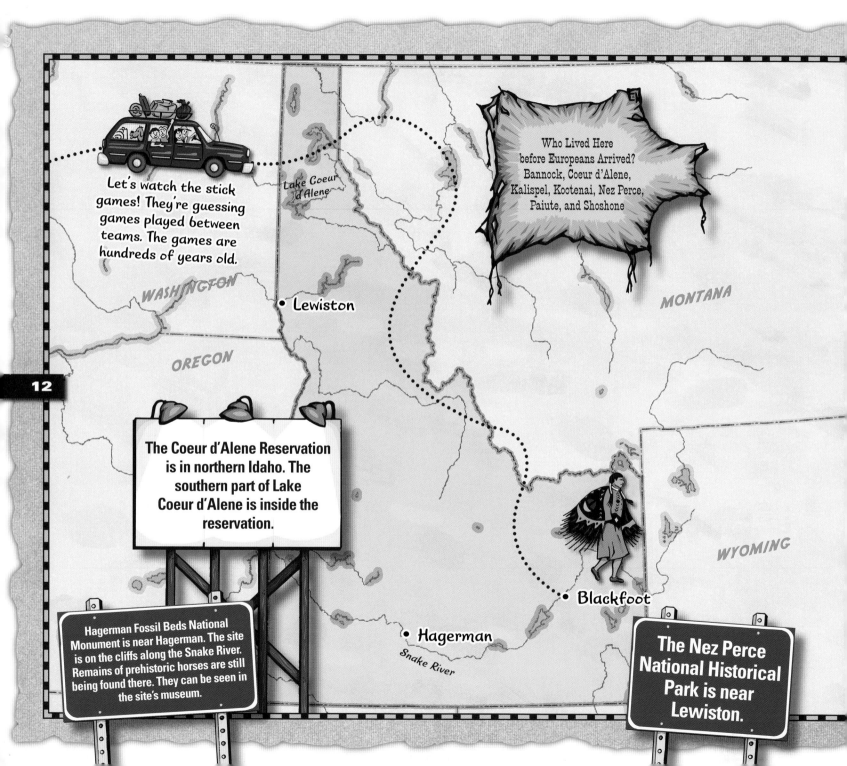

Let's watch the stick games! They're guessing games played between teams. The games are hundreds of years old.

Lake Coeur d'Alene

Who Lived Here before Europeans Arrived? Bannock, Coeur d'Alene, Kalispel, Kootenai, Nez Perce, Paiute, and Shoshone

WASHINGTON

• Lewiston

OREGON

MONTANA

12

The Coeur d'Alene Reservation is in northern Idaho. The southern part of Lake Coeur d'Alene is inside the reservation.

WYOMING

• Blackfoot

Hagerman Fossil Beds National Monument is near Hagerman. The site is on the cliffs along the Snake River. Remains of prehistoric horses are still being found there. They can be seen in the site's museum.

• Hagerman

Snake River

The Nez Perce National Historical Park is near Lewiston.

The Shoshone-Bannock Indian Festival

See the dancers in colorful beads and fringe. Watch the pony races and the all-Indian rodeo. You're enjoying the Shoshone-Bannock Indian Festival! It's on the Fort Hall **Reservation** near Blackfoot.

Many Native American groups once lived in Idaho. The Shoshone and Bannock were in the south. They built cone-shaped homes of grass or bark. They caught fish, rabbits, and other small animals. They also hunted for antelope, bison, deer, and elk.

Several groups lived in the north. The Nez Perce were one of the largest groups. They lived in longhouses. They caught salmon and other fish.

These Indians wear traditional dress. They're part of the Shoshone-Bannock Indian Festival.

Are we back in the 1800s? No, we're just visiting the Sacajawea Center in Salmon.

Lewis and Clark met Sacajawea in North Dakota. She traveled with them through Montana, Idaho, Washington, and Oregon.

Sacajawea's Birthplace

Meriwether Lewis and William Clark explored present-day Idaho in 1805. They were the first white people in the area. They were exploring westward across North America. They hoped to reach the Pacific Ocean. The Shoshone and Nez Perce helped the explorers.

A Shoshone woman joined them as a translator. Her name was Sacajawea. She could speak the local Indians' languages.

You'll learn all about Sacajawea in Salmon. Just visit the Sacajawea Interpretive, Cultural, and Education Center. It's in the Lemhi Valley, where Sacajawea was born. She returned there after helping Lewis and Clark.

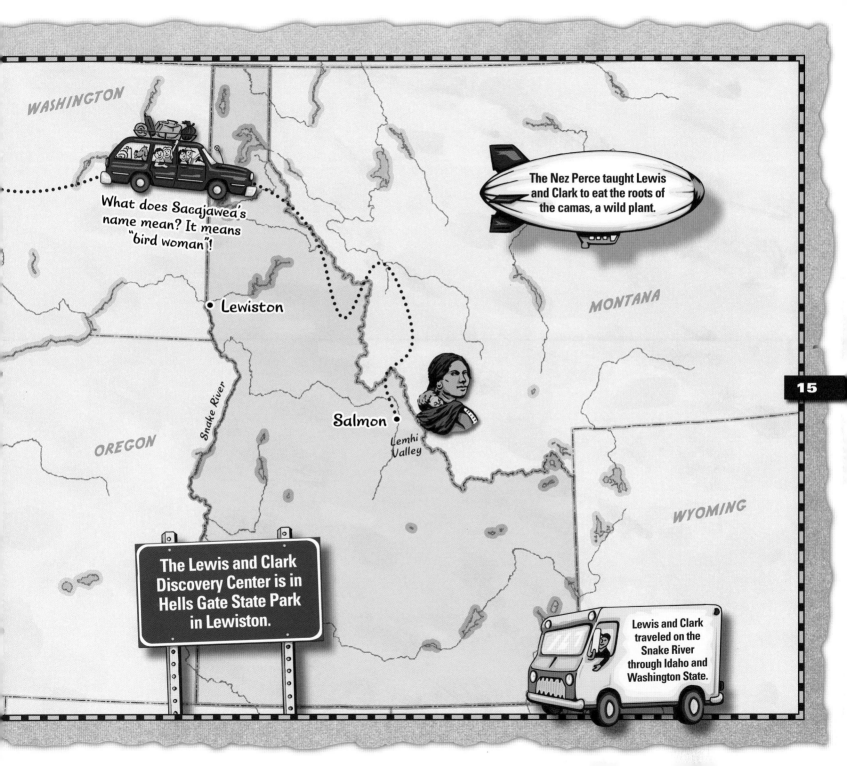

WASHINGTON

What does Sacajawea's name mean? It means "bird woman"!

The Nez Perce taught Lewis and Clark to eat the roots of the camas, a wild plant.

MONTANA

• Lewiston

Snake River

Salmon •

Lemhi Valley

OREGON

WYOMING

The Lewis and Clark Discovery Center is in Hells Gate State Park in Lewiston.

Lewis and Clark traveled on the Snake River through Idaho and Washington State.

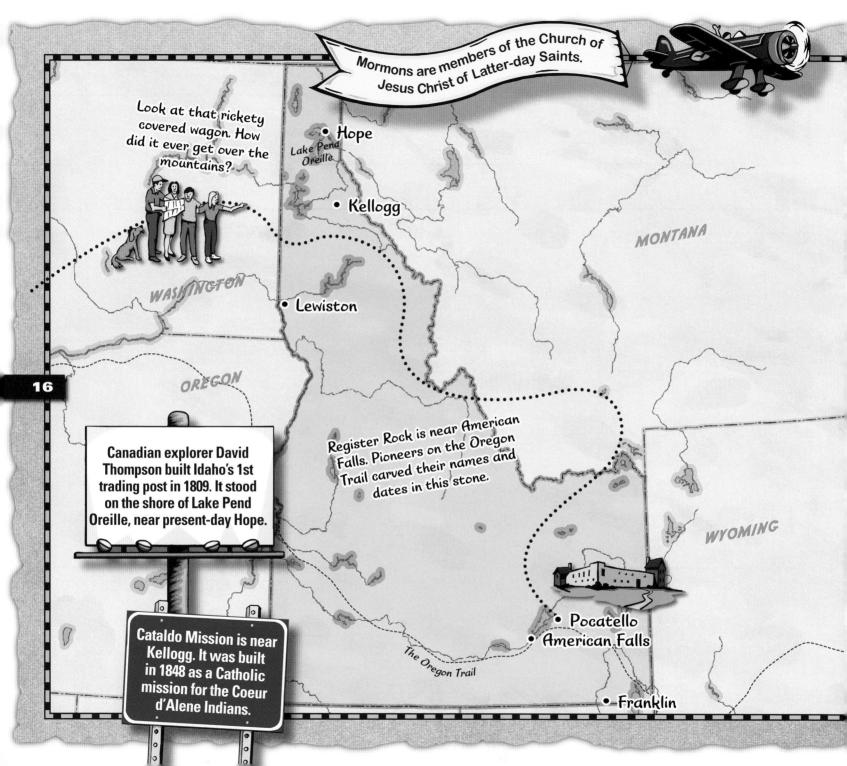

Mormons are members of the Church of Jesus Christ of Latter-day Saints.

Look at that rickety covered wagon. How did it ever get over the mountains?

Hope

Lake Pend Oreille

Kellogg

MONTANA

WASHINGTON

Lewiston

OREGON

Canadian explorer David Thompson built Idaho's 1st trading post in 1809. It stood on the shore of Lake Pend Oreille, near present-day Hope.

Register Rock is near American Falls. Pioneers on the Oregon Trail carved their names and dates in this stone.

WYOMING

Cataldo Mission is near Kellogg. It was built in 1848 as a Catholic mission for the Coeur d'Alene Indians.

The Oregon Trail

Pocatello

American Falls

Franklin

Old Fort Hall in Pocatello

Stroll around Old Fort Hall. This place has lots of memories. Weary trappers came here. Some were Indians, and some were white. They brought loads of animal furs. They stocked up on supplies. Then they headed back out into the wilderness.

Fur traders set up many trading posts in Idaho. Fort Hall was built in 1834. Soon it became a welcome stop for pioneers. They were traveling west along the Oregon Trail.

Christian **missionaries** built Lapwai Mission in 1836. It stood near Lewiston. Mormons came to Idaho, too. In 1860, they settled in Franklin. That was Idaho's first permanent town.

Would you have made a good pioneer? Visit Old Fort Hall and find out!

Old Fort Hall is a rebuilt site. The original Fort Hall was torn down.

Museum Comes to Life

Watch mountain men build fires with **flint.** Enjoy some music in the saloon. Stroll through an old-time log cabin. Pan for gold and rope a cow.

You're visiting Museum Comes to Life. That's a weekend festival in Boise. It takes place in the city's Pioneer Village. There you'll learn about pioneer life. You'll also test your pioneer skills.

Pioneer life in Idaho was rough. People built log cabins and made their own clothes. They hunted deer and other animals for food. Winters could be bitterly cold. People snuggled under wool blankets or furs. Could you have made it as a pioneer?

Giddy up! See an 1800s stagecoach at Museum Comes to Life.

Pioneers lit their homes with candles. They made the candles from animal fat.

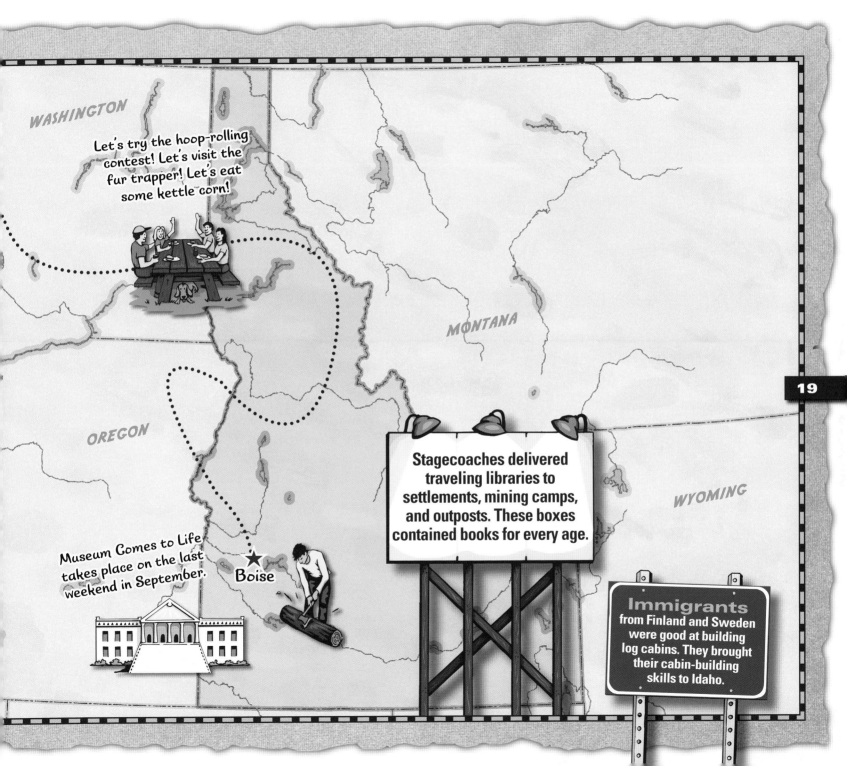

WASHINGTON

Let's try the hoop-rolling contest! Let's visit the fur trapper! Let's eat some kettle corn!

MONTANA

OREGON

Museum Comes to Life takes place on the last weekend in September.

★ Boise

WYOMING

Stagecoaches delivered traveling libraries to settlements, mining camps, and outposts. These boxes contained books for every age.

Immigrants from Finland and Sweden were good at building log cabins. They brought their cabin-building skills to Idaho.

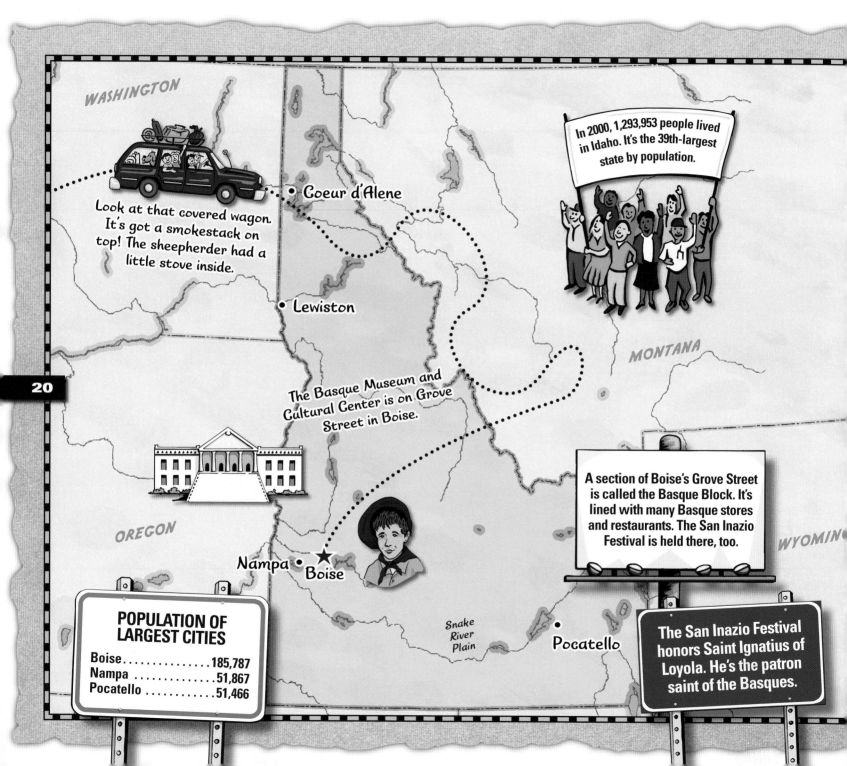

WASHINGTON

Look at that covered wagon. It's got a smokestack on top! The sheepherder had a little stove inside.

• Coeur d'Alene

• Lewiston

In 2000, 1,293,953 people lived in Idaho. It's the 39th-largest state by population.

MONTANA

The Basque Museum and Cultural Center is on Grove Street in Boise.

OREGON

A section of Boise's Grove Street is called the Basque Block. It's lined with many Basque stores and restaurants. The San Inazio Festival is held there, too.

WYOMING

Nampa • ★ Boise

POPULATION OF LARGEST CITIES

Boise 185,787
Nampa 51,867
Pocatello 51,466

Snake River Plain

• Pocatello

The San Inazio Festival honors Saint Ignatius of Loyola. He's the patron saint of the Basques.

Basques and the San Inazio Festival

Kick-dancing boys kick higher than their heads. Girls in red skirts dance the hoop dance. Sheepherders' wagons stand around a square. It's the San Inazio Festival in Boise!

Basque people hold this colorful festival every year. Their **ancestors** came from the mountainous region of northwestern Spain. Basque immigrants began arriving in the mid-1800s. Many worked as sheepherders.

Much of Idaho is very lightly settled. Why? Because the land is so mountainous and rough. Most Idahoans live in two areas. One is the Snake River Plain. The other is between Lewiston and Coeur d'Alene.

Kick up your heels! Dancers perform at the San Inazio Festival.

Most of Idaho's Native Americans belong to the Shoshone or Nez Perce tribes.

You can tour Crystal Gold Mine in Kellogg.

Grab your hard hat! It's time for a tour of the Sierra Silver Mine.

Idaho was the 43rd state to enter the Union. It joined on July 3, 1890.

Sierra Silver Mine in Historic Wallace

Put on your shiny yellow hard hat. Then head down into the silver mine. Your guide is a real miner. He shows how miners got the silver out.

You're touring Sierra Silver Mine. It's in the old mining town of Wallace.

Both silver and gold were discovered in Idaho. People found gold in 1860. Then silver was discovered in the 1870s. Wallace is in the Coeur d'Alene mining district. This region is often called Silver Valley.

Thousands of people rushed into Idaho. They hoped to get rich. Some did, but most did not. The towns they left are now **ghost towns.**

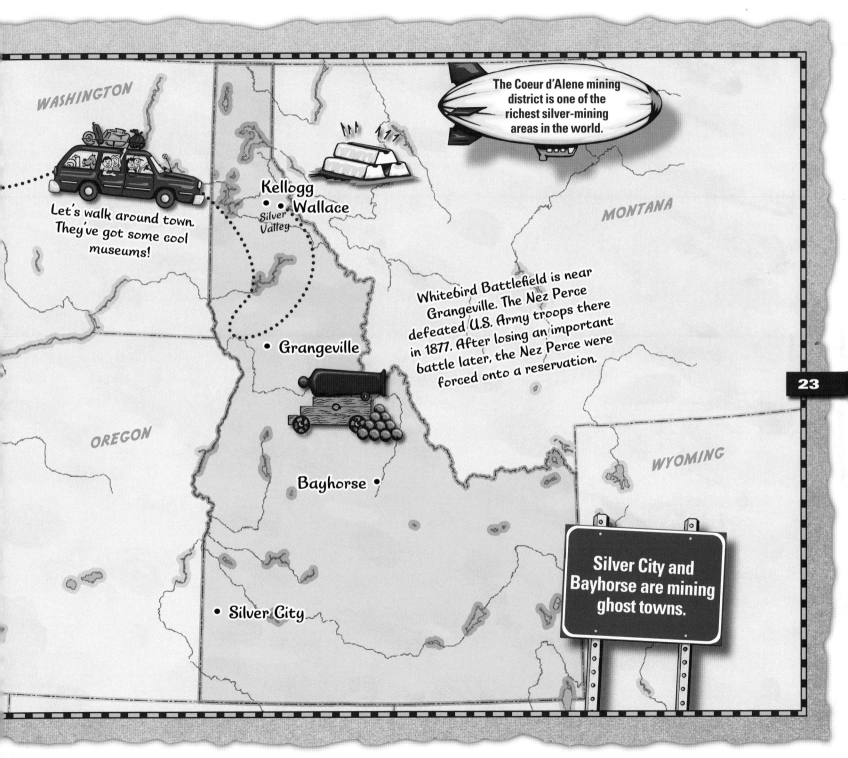

WASHINGTON

Let's walk around town. They've got some cool museums!

The Coeur d'Alene mining district is one of the richest silver-mining areas in the world.

MONTANA

Kellogg
Silver Valley
Wallace

Whitebird Battlefield is near Grangeville. The Nez Perce defeated U.S. Army troops there in 1877. After losing an important battle later, the Nez Perce were forced onto a reservation.

Grangeville

OREGON

WYOMING

Bayhorse

Silver City

Silver City and Bayhorse are mining ghost towns.

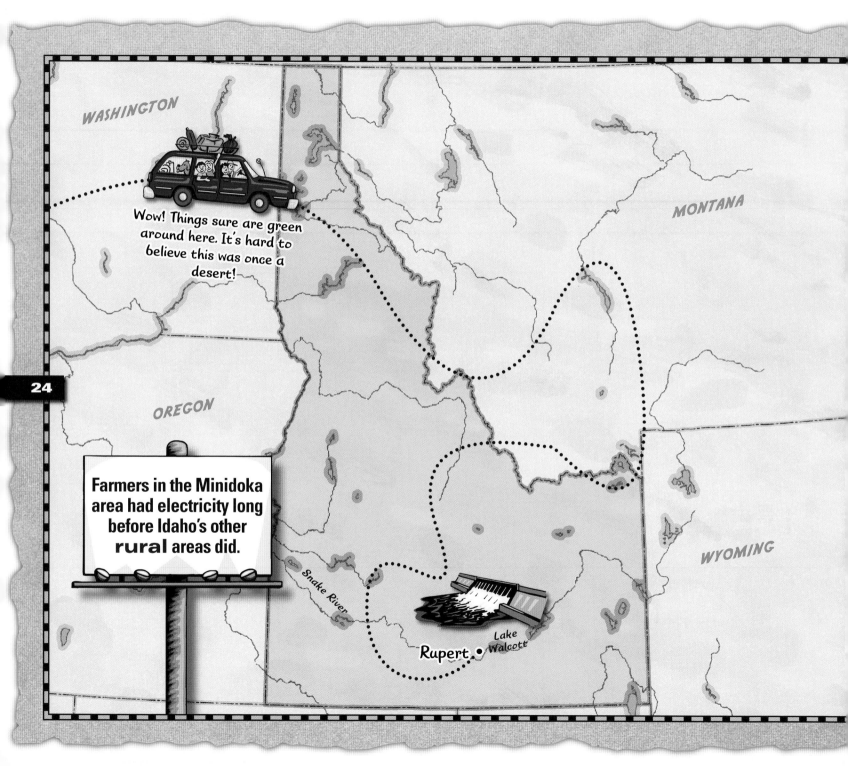

Wow! Things sure are green around here. It's hard to believe this was once a desert!

Farmers in the Minidoka area had electricity long before Idaho's other **rural** areas did.

WASHINGTON

MONTANA

OREGON

WYOMING

Snake River

Rupert • Lake Walcott

Minidoka Dam and Power Plant near Rupert

Look at the area around Rupert. This land gets very little rain. Yet it has some of Idaho's richest farmland. What makes this happen? Minidoka Dam!

This dam is on the Snake River. It opened in 1906. The dam holds back water, creating Lake Walcott. Water from the dam is directed through **canals.** From the canals, the water goes to farms. Near the dam is a power plant. It uses water power to create electricity.

Many other dams were built in Idaho. They are great for farmers. The dry land can now be used to grow lots of crops.

The Minidoka Dam creates scenic Lake Walcott.

Minidoka National Wildlife Refuge is near the dam. It has deer, antelope, eagles, ducks, and other wildlife.

25

Spud's the word! Try to take in an Idaho potato harvest.

Idaho is among the top 10 states for sheep, wool, lentils, milk, and cheese.

Pull that rope, and don't let go. Splat! You lose! You've landed in a pit of mashed potatoes! You're taking part in the big Spud Tug. This tug-of-war is messy but fun. It's just one event on Idaho Spud Day.

Spud Day celebrates Idaho's number-one crop. That's potatoes! Their nickname is spuds. No other state grows more potatoes.

Beef cattle are Idaho's most valuable farm product. Many farmers raise dairy cattle, too. Sheep are another valuable farm animal. They provide both wool and meat.

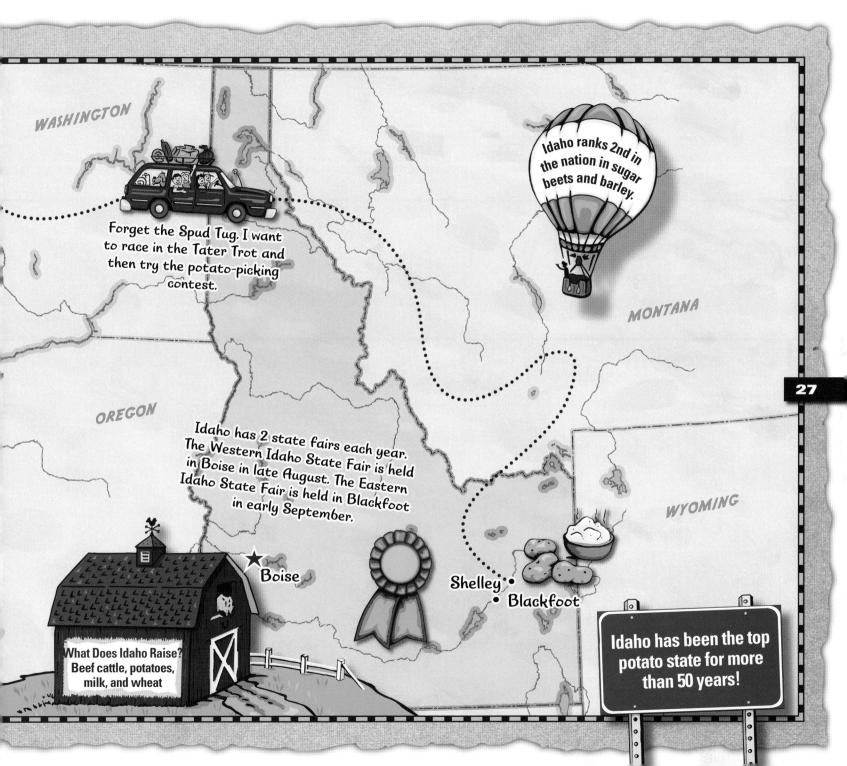

WASHINGTON

Idaho ranks 2nd in the nation in sugar beets and barley.

Forget the Spud Tug. I want to race in the Tater Trot and then try the potato-picking contest.

MONTANA

OREGON

Idaho has 2 state fairs each year. The Western Idaho State Fair is held in Boise in late August. The Eastern Idaho State Fair is held in Blackfoot in early September.

WYOMING

★ Boise

Shelley

Blackfoot

What Does Idaho Raise?
Beef cattle, potatoes, milk, and wheat

Idaho has been the top potato state for more than 50 years!

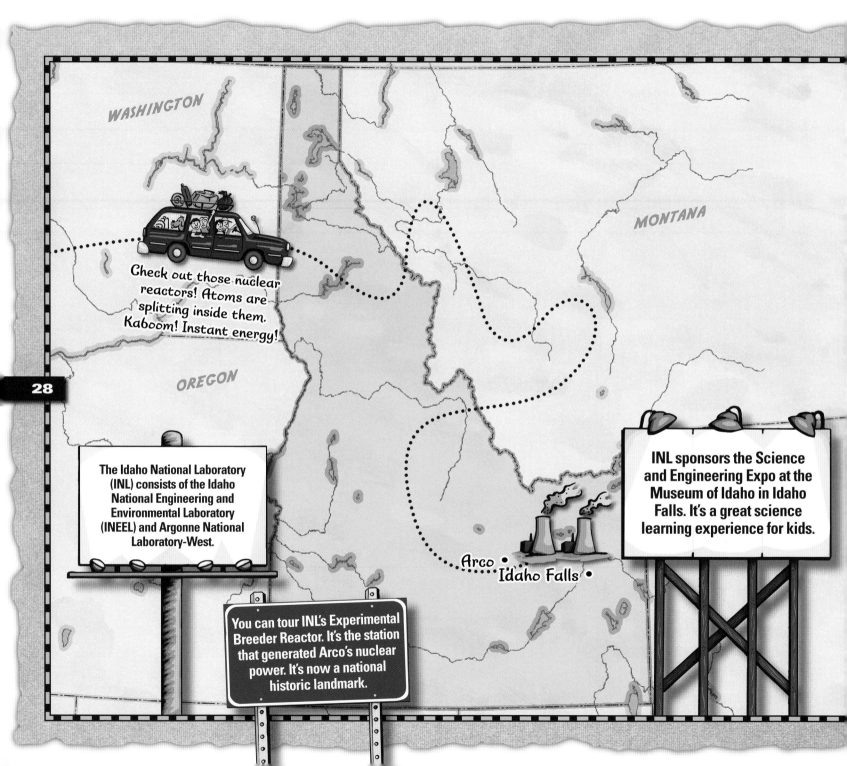

Check out those nuclear reactors! Atoms are splitting inside them. Kaboom! Instant energy!

The Idaho National Laboratory (INL) consists of the Idaho National Engineering and Environmental Laboratory (INEEL) and Argonne National Laboratory-West.

You can tour INL's Experimental Breeder Reactor. It's the station that generated Arco's nuclear power. It's now a national historic landmark.

INL sponsors the Science and Engineering Expo at the Museum of Idaho in Idaho Falls. It's a great science learning experience for kids.

WASHINGTON

MONTANA

OREGON

Arco •
Idaho Falls •

The Idaho National Laboratory

You've probably never heard of Arco. Many scientists know about it, though. In 1955, a nearby power plant geared up. It switched on Arco's electricity.

Why is this a big deal? Because the electricity came from **nuclear** energy. Arco became the world's first nuclear-powered city. The experiment was a success. Now thousands of cities use nuclear power.

The power plant opened in 1949. Now it's the Idaho National Laboratory (INL). It's between Arco and Idaho Falls. You can visit parts of the center. You'll see where they switched on Arco's lights!

Want to be a scientist someday? Head to the Idaho National Laboratory.

Idaho lawmakers are hard at work inside the capitol.

Hot water from deep underground is used to heat the capitol. No other state capitol is heated this way.

The State Capitol in Boise

Do you know anyone who's 100 years old? Idaho's capitol had its 100th birthday in 2005.

The capitol is a very important building. Inside are state government offices.

Idaho's state government has three branches. One branch has members from all over Idaho. They meet and make the state's laws. Another branch carries out the laws. It's headed by the governor. The third branch applies the laws. This branch is made up of judges. They decide whether someone has broken a law.

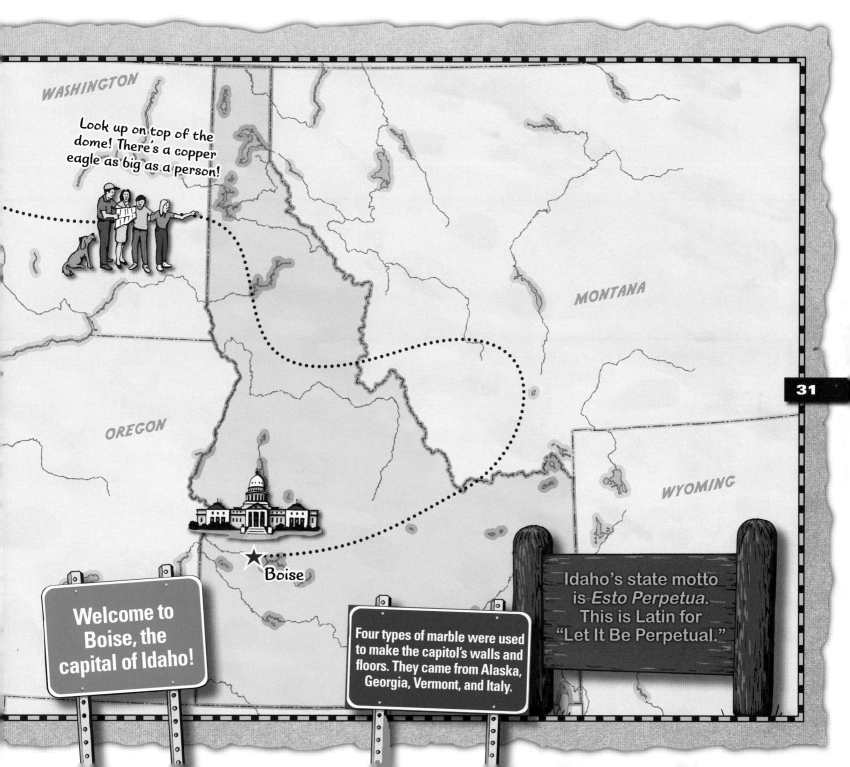

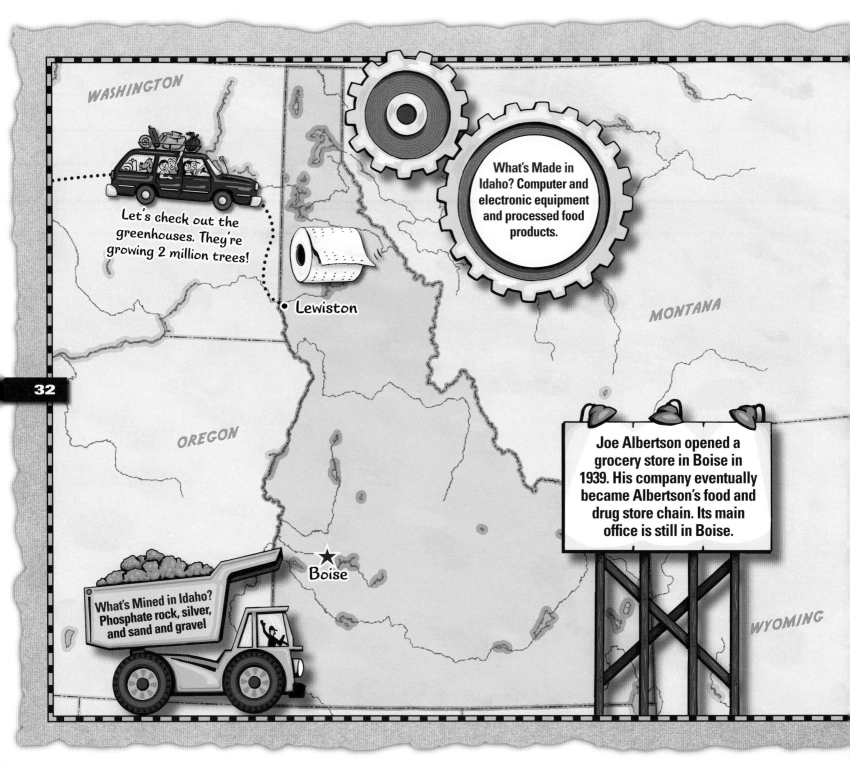